Dowsing
as a
Daily Tool

By
Robert Gandrup

SIXTH EDITION 2008

TABLE OF CONTENTS

What is Dowsing?

Dowsing is an age-old way to obtain information or physically locate any number of things. There are few cultures, past or present, that haven't used dowsing in some form.

In the Colonial U.S., people who used dowsing to find water were called water witches. They were highly regarded in the community but they were also feared because dowsing wasn't understood. The general belief of that time was that one had to have some magical powers to dowse, and the only ones who could use magic were witches.

Some of the finest minds of our time have understood the validity of dowsing. As Albert Einstein once said, "I know very well that many scientists consider dowsing as they do astrology, as a type of ancient superstition. According to my conviction this is, however, unjustified. The dowsing rod is a simple instrument which shows the reaction of the human nervous system to certain factors which are unknown to us at this time." Dowsing is accepted worldwide as a valid way to locate water or other underground items and has been studied extensively in what used to be the Soviet Union.

Today, many dowsers do more than just locate water. Some water dowsers actually move underground water veins to increase the productivity of a well or divert the flow away from an area where it would be detrimental. Prospectors are using it to detect minerals. It has been used to locate missing persons, but this can have less than satisfactory results if the person who is missing doesn't want to be found. There are dowsers that find and neutralize potentially harmful subtle energies in the home or workplace. It is sometimes used in conjunction with other practices such as Counseling or Feng Shui (the Chinese method of placing objects in your personal environment for positive effect).

There is an increasing interest in using dowsing for personal health. You can determine which vitamins to take or what foods would be good (or bad) for you. It can be used for relieving stress or to get an energy boost. There are ways to relieve aches and pains, **but this should be done with caution** because pain may be a symptom of illness or injury. Symptoms are what alert you to a problem so that it may be dealt with properly. Without the symptoms you may not be aware there was anything wrong. Don't try to use this as a substitute for proper medical treatment. There are other considerations in dowsing your health so this should not be done unless you are very skilled at dowsing and know its limitations and what it can truly offer. If you are experiencing a physical problem, be sure to consult a physician to see what treatments are available to you.

Perhaps the most interesting way to use dowsing is for spiritual growth and awareness. This is where the limits are defined only by the dowser's beliefs. Areas of growth and the ways to address these areas are easy to research. You can determine what kind of guidance or assistance is available to you and how to go about getting it.

The purpose of this book is to introduce you to the basic techniques so that you may incorporate dowsing into your daily life. You can use it for ordinary things such as choosing a restaurant or finding the proper location for a picture in your home. You can dowse new recipes when you're tired of eating the same old meals. On the other hand, you may want to use it in your work or to help with your spiritual awakening. There is no tool more versatile. It can be as much a part of your life as you want. The possibilities are infinite.

THE INSTRUMENTS

There are many different instruments (or devices) that can be used for dowsing and even more ways to use them. The following four are the most common and other instruments are usually a combination of several of these. Just because these instruments are the only ones mentioned here doesn't mean that they are the only ones or even the best ones to use. What you use doesn't matter at all as long as you can decipher a response from its motion. There is a fifth "instrument" mentioned in this book called *deviceless dowsing*. That is merely dowsing without the use of a physical tool to monitor your responses.

Y-ROD

 This is the traditional instrument used for water dowsing. It was originally a forked stick but there are many ways to make one using modern materials. It is held pointed up and out from the chest in both hands, palms up. Pressure is applied by rotating one's hands inward. A dowser turns in a circle while holding the y-rod in this manner. It dips down to indicate the direction to the water or item sought. Holding it up again, he then walks in the indicated direction and it will dip down as the item is reached. The Y-rod is effective but can be a bit difficult for beginners.

BOBBER

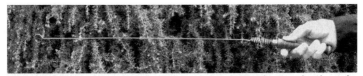

The bobber is a long wire or springy branch that is held (with one or both hands depending on the dowser's preference) at one end and pointed forward away from the body. There are several good ways to make one, depending on the sensitivity desired. This instrument can be anything that will spring up & down or side to side when held properly. A few of the things that make a good bobber are a piece of welding rod, a length of fence wire, a straight young shoot, a piece of speedometer cable or a radio antenna from a car. The response from this device can be an up and down or sideways motion. It can also circle either way.

L-RODS

These are two pieces of welding rod or other stiff wire bent in the shape of an "L". They are usually held, one in each hand, with the long end pointing forward. The response is seen as the rods rotate left or right in the dowser's hands. Typically, crossing toward each other is an affirmative and spreading apart is a negative answer. They can also point a direction to follow. Often the short side of the "L" is fitted with a piece of tubing to allow it to rotate easily in the dowser's hand.

PENDULUM

This is the most versatile and one of the easiest instruments to use. A pendulum can be anything suspended on a chain, strap or cord. The cord is then held in one hand allowing the weight to hang so that it  is free to swing in any direction. The response is the way the pendulum swings; forward and backward, side to side, circling, etc. The pendulum can also be used to trace lines, indicate a direction or point to something on a flat surface. This is particularly good for dowsing on maps or researching from lists, charts or other graphic representations. The pendulum is also the most portable instrument, being easy to carry in a pocket or purse.

DEVICELESS DOWSING

This needs mentioning since it is a valid and accurate way of dowsing, although few can do this without a lot of practice. With this method, the dowser uses his body as the instrument. This skill is generally developed after a dowser has become fairly proficient and notices a body reaction as he gets his answer with one of the other instruments. A muscle reflex or sensation in the body is a common indicator but it could be any number of things. The ultimate reaction is simply an inner knowing. Sounds a lot like intuition, doesn't it? A good way to think of dowsing is *intuition on demand*. Some dowsers don't need to use a pendulum or other device but choose to use one as a focal item. Having something to concentrate on makes it easier to ignore any distractions going on around you. The use of an instrument as a focal tool varies greatly from one person to another and falls into the category of personal preference.

Many consider the pendulum as the primary dowsing instrument. This book focuses on it because it is versatile and easily carried. The techniques explained in this book are universal and can be used with any tool other than the way an instrument moves and the resultant response it can give.

THE MENTAL STATE

Your state of mind is very important to dowsing. This is not referring to your sanity, rather the frame of mind you should achieve to get good, accurate  dowsing. To do this, your mind must be clear and free of your own conscious intervention. The less you are involved with the results of the issue, the easier it is to get correct responses. When you are involved with the outcome, it is hard to get answers that are free of your own conscious or subconscious intervention. Remember that your subconscious will try to provide you with what you want and if you really want to see a particular answer, your subconscious will strive to provide that for you. For this reason, it can be extremely hard to dowse regarding your own health or pertaining to issues where you have a vested interest in the outcome. I've seen new dowsers immediately start trying to figure out a serious health problem and they lack the experience to do so correctly. Even after years of practice, it can be difficult to dowse some issues clearly. Dowsing has no limits but we, as people, do. We live in a society that doesn't embrace dowsing as a normal practice and that is the hardest thing for many of us to overcome. Dowsing is a learned skill, just like flying an airplane or doing dental work. You wouldn't buy

12

a new unicycle and ride it across the Grand Canyon on a wire without some practice, especially if you have never ridden one before. Exercise some common sense regarding this and practice every day to improve your skills before tackling serious issues.

Your conscious mind can also adversely effect your dowsing accuracy by evaluating the messages from your subconscious then intervening with the dowsing response to give you the answer you would like to see. Without any left-brain activity, the response will be unedited, direct from your subconscious mind. Some of the factors that can lead to conscious intervention are:

• Wanting to get a particular response.
• Preconceived opinions or feelings of what the answer should be.
• Fear or doubt regarding your own ability to dowse.
• Anger or any other negative emotion.
• Mental fatigue or any factor that can prevent your being able to reach the Alpha mental state.
• Not regarding dowsing as a valid practice.

When dowsing, you need to be clear of all mental clutter and focused on the questions without being involved with the answers. If you can achieve this, you will get consistently accurate answers.

Dowsing works when the dowser's mind is slightly into the Alpha, or meditative, state. Anyone who meditates generally finds dowsing easy to do because the mental skills are similar. For this same reason, dowsing can make meditating easier because it gets one used to quieting the mind to receive messages from the subconscious. It should be noted here that prayer also utilizes this same state so if you don't identify with meditating, use the same frame of mind as when praying.

To achieve the slight alpha state, close your eyes and relax. You're there. That is the simple way to achieve it. After you have a feel for that and can identify the inner calm and connection with your eyes closed, open them and maintain that same mental state. It may help to defocus your eyes slightly at first until you get used to it. Eventually, you will be able to get into the proper mental state by simply relaxing and going to it. This may take a little time at first, but soon you will be doing it in a few seconds or less without closing your eyes.

THE WAY IT WORKS

The dowsing instruments are nothing more than a way to bypass the myriad of thoughts, images and pre-conceived ideas that are generated by the conscious mind. When you dowse, the conscious mind formulates a question and presents it to the subconscious. The subconscious mind, eager to please, gets the answer for you. The subconscious is very familiar with running your body without you needing to do anything. Since it doesn't have the ability to open the line of communication to the conscious mind, it bypasses all the conscious activity and does what it can to get your attention: it tweaks your muscles, generating a response in your pendulum or other instrument.

All the dowsing instrument does is monitor the minute movements of your muscles. The item you use for dowsing has absolutely no power or intrinsic energy of its own, nor does it act like an antenna or any other receiving apparatus. If you were to hang a weight from the limb of a tree on a cord, when the wind moved the upper branches of the tree the weight would move from the small amount of transferred motion in the larger limb. Your dowsing  instrument is the same. Don't assign it any power.

There is a man I met who thinks he has to respect his pendulum or it won't work. It is kept wrapped in a black silk cloth, out of the sunlight, safe in the bottom of a drawer. If another person handles it, there is a whole involved procedure for neutralizing the energies it picks up so the thing will work again. This is all unnecessary since the dowsing instrument is just a tool, like a screwdriver or a hammer.

Does your arm really move? Certainly, but if your attention is focused on the instrument it will appear to move on it's own. An experienced dowser's arm may move considerably but he is seldom conscious of it. All you need to do is ask a question then let your subconscious do what it does best. The result is your answer.

DEFINING YOUR RESPONSES

Before you can expect to get understandable answers, you must first establish what various motions of the pendulum (or any instrument, for that matter) will mean. For example, most people like a fore and aft swing to mean "Yes" and a side-to-side swing to mean "No". There really isn't a right or wrong way to have it. All that matters is for you to define what you want for your responses so you know what the instrument's motion is indicating. In this section, you will learn how to program the responses you want to see so that every time you start dowsing, you know what to expect and how to interpret the responses. You can use the following defined responses or any others of your choosing. The most important issue is that the responses make sense to you. If you use your own, follow the same basic procedure to define yours. The following definitions are one way to use a pendulum.

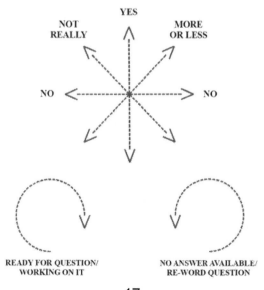

17

"YES" and "NO"

To program your subconscious for a "Yes", hold the pendulum string between your thumb and forefinger with the pendulum hanging on about 2 to 4 inches of string. Hold it out in front of you with your arm relaxed, the elbow pointing down and your forearm extending forward. Don't hold your arm against your body, as this tends to dampen the response. Relax and clear your mind of as much conscious activity as you can. Gently swing the pendulum forward and backward and tell your subconscious that this motion is what you want to be a "Yes" response. Next, stop the pendulum and tell your subconscious to show you a "Yes". The pendulum should seemingly start swinging on it's own. If it doesn't, relax then try the process again. If you still don't get any motion from the pendulum try again later.

Once you get the desired "Yes" response, program your subconscious for the side to side "No" response using the technique you used to program your "Yes". Once that is done, do the following responses the same way.

"MORE OR LESS" and "NOT REALLY"

Sometimes you ask a question that can't be answered with either a "Yes" or a "No". In that case, you need a response for something that is somewhere in between. For "Not Really", use a 45° swing to the left, and for "More or Less", a 45° swing to the right (see the illustration on the previous page).

"READY FOR QUESTION"

When you are asking a question, your pendulum needs to be giving no response at all or, even better, already be in motion but not as it would be for one of your pre-defined responses. It is easier for your subconscious to convert one motion into another one than to initiate a motion from a still condition. For a neutral or "Ready for Question" response, program your subconscious to use a gentle clockwise circling of the pendulum.

"WORKING ON IT"

There are times when your subconscious is working on obtaining the information, but a little time will be involved before you get an answer. For this "Working on it" response, use a continuous clockwise circling to then be followed by the appropriate answer. If you ask a question and the pendulum continues to circle clockwise, this shows that you will get the answer as soon as it is available. If you don't get your answer in a short time, dowse how long the answer will take.

"NO ANSWER AVAILABLE"

There may be times when your question is not clear and needs to be re-worded, the answer to your question is not available or the answer shouldn't be given to you. In these instances it is good to have a response for "No Answer Available" or "Not going to Answer". The response for this should be a counter-clockwise circling of the pendulum.

"STOP QUESTIONING"

Occasionally, your Higher Self may need to tell you to stop or change your line of questioning. To indicate this "Stop Questioning" response, program your subconscious to have the pendulum hang straight down with no motion at all.

If your responses seem weak or barely perceptible after programming them, tell your subconscious to increase the amount of swing until it is to your liking. If all you can get is a slight motion, don't worry because that will work just fine. As you get more practiced, the motions will gradually become more pronounced.

CHOOSING A PENDULUM

The pendulum you select is entirely a matter of your likes and dislikes. What it is made of is irrelevant. You can use a washer tied on a string or a $500 one made of crystal or gold with a hand-made chain but the result is the same. All you need is something that will swing and give you a response. Beyond that, it is a matter of preference. There are pendulums with a hollow center so the dowser can put a sample, called a *witness*, of what he is looking for inside. This is fine but it doesn't affect the way the pendulum works other than as determined by the belief system of the dowser. If you believe you need to have a sample to correctly dowse, then that will be the case. Be careful you don't get too much into the process and mystique of the pendulum and miss the point of it being simply a tool to be used. You can chrome plate a hammer, but it won't be any better for driving nails than one that has no plating.

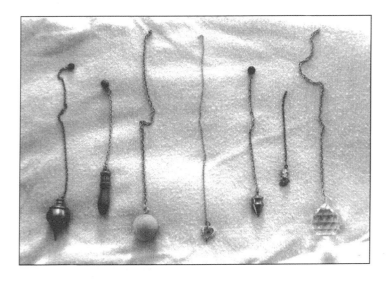

There are a couple of considerations that affect the speed and swing of your pendulum. One is how much string or chain should there be between your hand and the weight, or *bob*, as it is called. This is entirely up to the dowser's preference. With a longer the string, the pendulum will react slower but have more definite responses. A shorter string will give a quicker response but the motion will be less. Another factor that will affect the response of your pendulum is how heavy the bob is. A heavier one will react slower but give more defined responses and be less susceptible to being blown by the wind if you are working outside. Play with different length strings and weights to see which you like best. If you have a pendulum you are particularly fond of, use it.

There are times when you need to dowse a location on a map or select one answer from a list of possibilities. Many dowsers like a pendulum that has a point on it for this purpose. As with all aspects of choosing your pendulum, this is purely a matter of preference. The use of charts will be covered in detail later.

Before Asking Your Questions

There are several things that must be done *EVERY TIME* you dowse. This doesn't mean before each question, but certainly at the beginning of a session even if you are going to ask only one question. Neglecting to do these simple steps can lead to erroneous answers.

FIRST - Surround yourself with light. White light is best because it includes every color and vibration. Use it with two intents: (1) to help you to get centered and tuned-in to your Higher Self, and (2) to protect you from outside interference such as conscious or unconscious intervention from other people, thought forms or entities other than your own guides.

SECOND - Relax and get into the mild Alpha state and separate yourself from the issue you are dowsing. In this state you can still function normally and carry on conversations. Remember: after you ask the question, your conscious mind should be an observer rather than a participant in the process of obtaining information.

THIRD - There are three basic questions that you should ask prior to dowsing on a subject. If you change subjects or if you suspect perhaps you shouldn't continue with a particular line of questioning, ask them again. These questions are:

- *Can I?* This is to find out if you have the skill and ability to properly dowse about the intended subject and if you are ready with your mind clear enough to do so.

23

- *May I?* With this question, you find out if you have the appropriate permission to continue. This permission comes from the Unified Field, the Infinite Being, God, Allah, the Great Goombah, or whatever name your belief system calls it.

- *Should I?* This question is the most important. Since you are created with free will, you may be given permission to do something you have the ability to do but that really shouldn't be done. The reason may not be obvious so just be satisfied that there is a good one. Life is for learning, and you have been given the ability to choose. Do so wisely. It's like setting a bucket of water on a tree limb with a rope tied to the handle, then handing it to someone and saying, "You shouldn't pull on that rope, but it's up to you."

The question "Should I?" is particularly important when dowsing issues concerning others. DON'T PRY INTO OTHER PEOPLE'S LIVES; your dowsing will almost certainly be inaccurate if you do. If you are going to dowse regarding another person, be sure you have a genuine need to know the information you seek. Being nosey isn't in anyone's best interest and serves no useful purpose, therefore it doesn't qualify as a genuine need to know.

If you get a "No" to one of these three questions, don't dowse it at that time. If it's important, try again later; conditions change and you may be able to do it then.

When you dowse, you can combine these three questions into one; "Can I, May I and Should I ...?" If you get a "Yes" this applies to all three. If the answer is a "No", a "Not really", a "More or less" or anything other than a definite "Yes", don't proceed. When you don't get the go-ahead to dowse, don't even try to determine why unless you suspect that the intended questioning might not be addressing the subject correctly. If this happens, dowse until you find what the problem is, then ask again. If you then get a "Yes" be sure to avoid questioning in the manner that gave you the "No" response before.

ASKING QUESTIONS

Can I?

May I?

Should I?

The most important part of accurate dowsing is asking the right question. Most often when answers seem erroneous or odd, it's usually that the question was not specific enough. Your subconscious is extremely literal. If you ask a question that can be interpreted several ways, your chances of getting the right answer are reduced.

Let's say you're in the bookstore and pick up a book on numerology. If you ask, "Is this a good book?" your answer may be a "Yes" if you are interested in it or if it had information that was accurate. If you don't believe that numerology works, your answer might be a "No". Perhaps at this time in your life you think it's all a bunch of superstitious nonsense, but next year you could decide to study numerology to see if it really has some validity. Again, there are two possible answers. If it's a fairly sizable book and all you need is a doorstop, the answer could be "Yes". Also, what is good for you may not be good for someone else. A better way to ask the question would be, "Would I benefit by reading this book at this time?" The more specific and less subjective your question is, the more accurate your answer will be.

Two people can ask the same question and get very different answers. The wording may be slightly different as each person asks it. Even if the wording is the same, it may mean something different to another person. At night, if you ask an astronomer the question "Is the sun shining?" he may say "Yes," because he thinks of the Earth as a sphere and somewhere the sun is shining on it. If he's thinking about the fact that the sun radiates rather than reflects light, he might say "No".

Don't make your questions too complex. Be sure that you aren't asking multiple questions. For example, "Is this a good pen for calligraphy and will I be happy with it?" covers two very different ideas. You must be clear and specific about what you want to ask. If your question is vague or general, your subconscious will give you the most correct answer, but the result is an answer with the potential to be completely wrong. If you change the question in your mind while you are asking it, your answer could be for the wrong question. Be careful to word your question to mean exactly and only what you want. It helps to write a question down so that you have it already formulated.

A question like "Would I be happy living in Denver?" covers a lot of information. You might like the people, but not the weather. The cost of living may be better than what you are used to, but there may not be any jobs available for you. It is better to break the question down to the simplest elements and ask those individually. Is there employment available to me in Denver that I would enjoy doing? Is the wage level in Denver high enough to support the type of lifestyle I am used to enjoying? Are the people in Denver the type I would like having for neighbors? Will I have the type of social life I am used to in Denver? If there are aspects that don't matter to you, don't bother asking about them.

Ask questions that can be answered with hard facts. The information available to you is just that: information. Opinions or hunches aren't anything that you will be able to get through dowsing. It is best to define exactly what you need to know and ask questions that will have factual answers.

Your questions need to have a reference. "Will this car give me good service?" is a question that has no reference. What is the definition of "good"? The question, "Will this car be as good, mechanically, as my old Chrysler?" is comparing the new car to your old Chrysler. Whether the old car was a great one or a lemon will affect the answer, but it's a reference and can be used for a comparison.

It is difficult to accurately dowse the future because it's always changing. Since we all have free will, everything everyone does affects coming events. The future can never be determined beyond how things are at the moment you ask the question, then as conditions change, your answer becomes out of date. If conditions change very little, you may find your dowsing to have been accurate. On the other hand, if conditions change a lot, what you dowsed before may be very different than what actually transpires. I had a man explain to me that he dowsed he would see a certain person, who he had not seen in years, during a two-week period nine months in the future. The time period came and went and he didn't meet the person. He did, however, run into the person in a store a couple of days after the end of his two-week window. "What did I do wrong?" he asked. In my opinion, he did better than could be expected. In fact, it's possible that during the two-week period that person had driven by in a car but the man didn't recognize him. In that case, he would have been right on with his dowsing. If conditions don't change much, you can get answers that prove to have been accurate, but that is not something that can be considered reliable dowsing. All you can hope to dowse is what will be as conditions are **at the time of your dowsing** and that will only be accurate if conditions don't change.

As mentioned before, you must have a genuine need to know the answer or your dowsing won't work properly. Stay to business that concerns you. Also, dowsing isn't a game but if you treat it like one, your answers will be in keeping with a game: worthless in real life. How do you get to practice? Developing your dowsing skills is a genuine need to get correct answers so when you practice, do it with the intent of becoming proficient rather than doing it simply for entertainment. That puts your dowsing in the category of a genuine need. Start by dowsing things that aren't of great importance to you and it will be easier to keep your conscious mind from interfering. A good way to practice is to ask questions that easily allow you to remain detached from the outcome. What color clothes to wear, what to plant in your garden, which book you would enjoy reading the most or other questions of this nature are excellent. Dowsing this type of information has a very real value so you can start using it in your daily life immediately. The more you dowse, the more proficient you get and as you get better at it you will find an increasing number of ways to use it.

When you have finished dowsing, it is advisable that you always ask one last question to see if there is anything that you have missed. Ask something like "Is there anything else I need to know about this subject?" If there is, keep dowsing until you get a "No" to your ending question.

A friend of mine asked me if I could help clear up the water in her home. She had a well that was so high in iron content that the water wasn't fit to drink. Even after running it through double filters it had a murky brown color. I found that diverting a contaminated vein away from the well and bringing in two smaller ones to make up for the loss of volume could clear up the water. I checked to see that the new veins were good potable water and proceeded to make the corrections. When the water was analyzed, the iron content had gone down to almost nothing. During the same time, however, the manganese content went way up. After checking, I found that one of the new veins had picked up manganese getting to the well. To correct this, I re-diverted the one new vein back to its original course and brought in another one. This time I asked if the water would be good, potable water when it got to the well. That took care of the problem. Before, when I reduced the iron content, I'd forgotten to ask if there was anything else I needed to know before making any corrections. Had I done so, I would have eventually determined that one new vein would pick up some contaminants on the way to the well. Remember that important last question!

Know exactly what you want to ask, be specific, keep it simple and ask questions that have factual answers. If you are too close to the issue to be objective, ask the help of someone who has been dowsing for a while and is good at getting accurate answers. While you are learning don't get too wrapped up in the need to have perfect results immediately. Relax and take things as they come. With a little practice you will become a skilled dowser.

DOWSING CHARTS

Charts are a good way to determine one answer from a bunch of different possibilities without going through the strokes of asking, "Is this it?" for each one. To quickly select the most appropriate answer to your question, you can list all your options on a chart and dowse from that list.

For example, lets say you lost your keys and need to find them. They could be in any room of your house. There are a finite number of rooms so you can list all of them on  a piece of paper. That list becomes your chart. Turn the list sideways and have your pendulum point to the appropriate one for your answer.

For charts you are going to use repeatedly, you can make a permanent chart. A fan chart is good for this because the pendulum swings from the center to point to the appropriate answer. To use this type of chart, hold your pendulum so that it is hanging over the point at the bottom of the fan where the rays meet. Ask which answer is the most appropriate and your pendulum will swing in the direction of the right one. This will work for anything that has up to about 15 or so possible answers. Beyond that, it gets a little difficult to identify exactly which answer is indicated since they are so close together.

A fan chart can be simply visualized rather than written down, provided you can keep track of what is at each point. You can make charts to cover whatever information you need. In the back of this book you will find a larger copy of a fan chart and some other examples of charts including a couple of blank ones that you can copy or write on for future use.

BALANCING & CLEARING

Your pendulum can be used as a monitor for balancing your chakras (the seven basic energy centers in your body), aura, and other body systems. Similarly, some dowsers have found it useful for clearing blocks in your life such as fears, anger, resentment, or other negative emotions or programs that can prevent you from successfully accomplishing your life purpose.

Research thoroughly before doing any of this type of work to make sure you know exactly what needs to be done. When you feel you know what to do, be sure to ask if there is anything else you need to know before proceeding. Once you have all the information you need, hold the pendulum in the same manner as when you are about to dowse. Instruct your subconscious to begin the clearing or balancing and to circle the pendulum clockwise (the waiting or searching response) the whole time, notifying you when it has been completed by giving a fore and aft, or "Yes", response (you can specify any pendulum motion for the indicator that the work is done but most use the affirmative response). When finished, always ask if everything was done correctly and completely. If not, do the work again.

Before I start this process, I always dowse how long it will take. If it will be more than a minute or two, I ask my subconscious if the clearing or balancing can be done without my needing to hold the pendulum the entire time. If it can, I instruct my subconscious to begin then go about my business and check after the time is up to see if the task is completed.

This technique has many applications. It's simple and it causes you to put your attention on the task at hand. In quantum physics, things come into being only when you put your attention on them. It seems that this may apply to the way we function, as well.

HEALTH

It has been my experience that every physical problem has its roots in some sort of learning situation. I feel that all illness or injury is a condition that has an underlying reason on a spiritual level. As a dowser, you can determine what the learning experience is by asking questions until you narrow it down. For example, an illness that had a long recovery time requiring a lot of bedside assistance might be a lesson in accepting help from others. Understanding what you need to learn from a situation can make your life lesson much easier.

When researching in the area of health, be careful that you don't let some ailment go untreated. When you find a spiritual cause for a problem, that doesn't mean it will disappear on the physical level. Dowsing is not a method of treatment, and finding the underlying cause is not a substitute for the attention of a licensed practitioner. If the engine in your car started knocking and you found that it was low on oil, the cause of the problem would have been the lack of oil. Simply eliminating the cause by filling it with oil wouldn't change the fact that it still had damage that would need to be repaired by a mechanic. However, you most likely would learn to keep oil in it so it didn't happen again.

Use dowsing to help you identify the underlying spiritual cause for a physical problem so that you can properly address the lesson in it. If you can eliminate the need for the problem, you may make it easier for treatment to be effective. Your dowsing should be an aid to, not a substitute for, proper care.

A LAST WORD

Treat your dowsing like every other part of your life. It doesn't take any special talent or magical power. It's a skill that anyone can develop. Like any skill, it will take some practice to get really good at it. Some people may take more time to perfect it but everyone has the ability. It isn't a matter of intelligence or physical aptitude. You just have to learn how to formulate and ask the proper questions then allow your body to show you the answers.

You can buy all different kinds of pendulums and other dowsing instruments made from a variety of materials. Keep in mind that the dowsing tool has no special power or influence of it's own. The instrument can be anything. The real power is you. *You* ask the questions and *you* get the answers. The dowsing instrument is moved by *you*. Some dowsers believe they need a special device or a particular ritual to make dowsing work. For them, this is true because that is what they choose to believe.

Keep it simple. You will most likely have a particular pendulum (or other instrument) that you prefer to use. It's like choosing a car or pen, pick one that pleases you. I have my favorite but anything will work. If I want to use a pendulum while hiking and didn't bring one, a stick suspended by a strand of moss will do just fine. For a bobber, a small, springy branch will fill the need. In my home or garage, there are many things available to make a wide variety of good dowsing tools. Choose to be unlimited with your dowsing. You decide your own reality so make it what you want. If it works for you then it's right and proper.

Always use your dowsing skills for the greatest good of all concerned. Just as a carpenter can use his tools to build a home to improve the quality of life for a family, you can use this tool to improve the quality of your life and the lives of others. Intent is the most important single aspect of dowsing. With wrongful intent you will lose the 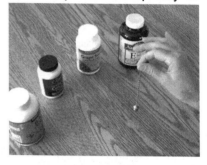 ability to dowse correctly. I've seen experienced dowsers start working away on a topic that is of no concern to them and the responses they get are totally incorrect. For some reason, when we get into a negative frame of mind, accuracy seems to go completely away. If you are genuinely using your skills to improve life for all concerned, the rewards can be far greater than you could imagine.

Dowsing for your needs, or the needs of others, is a good way to use this skill. What color a friend can wear to feel successful at work, the kind of job that would suit you, what would be good to have for dinner when guests come over, what vehicle will best serve your needs, or any other questions that will assist you on your life path are excellent uses for dowsing. Greed is one of the least justifiable reasons to use your skills; dowsing purely for profit doesn't work. If we could determine lottery numbers there would be nothing but rich dowsers in the world. Save yourself the aggravation and don't bother. This doesn't mean that you can't use this in your business or work, just be sure that your intent is for the greatest good of all concerned.

As already mentioned, don't pry into the lives of others. What is going on in another person's life is not your concern. If someone asks you to dowse for him or her, or if you have offered to do so and the offer was accepted, by all means, do it. In addition, the person who you are dowsing for should have a legitimate reason for asking your assistance. Otherwise, stay out of other people's affairs. Curiosity, nosiness or meddling does not represent a genuine interest. Always remember to ask the three basic questions before you start: "Can I, May I, Should I?" and act accordingly.

Never try to use dowsing to manipulate others or to interfere with someone's life purpose. If you do, you are opening yourself to all kinds of negative energies, Karmic debts or other problems.

Don't dowse to diagnose any physical ailments or illnesses, or to prescribe any kind of treatment or remedy. Instead, recommend that the person seek help from a proper health-care professional if he or she feels that there may be a problem. This is also true for any other practice that requires a license to treat or advise others. In addition, giving medical or other professional advice to others where you aren't licensed and properly qualified can cause legal problems for you.

Take your dowsing seriously, but don't get somber. We are all here to learn, but we are also meant to enjoy life. Nothing is more joyful or satisfying than personal growth and that's really what this is all about. There are an infinite number of ways to use dowsing. Use your imagination. See what ways you can find to apply this skill. Most importantly, have fun with it.

Sample Dowsing Charts

The following are examples that show how charts can be used. They aren't intended to be complete although you may find one or more useful. They're included to give you ideas on designing your own. The last two are blank so they can be copied to fill in as you choose. You may find it better to enlarge them when you make copies so they're easier to use.

BASIC FAN CHART

This chart covers the basic colors (including black which really isn't a color at all). Instead of colors, these could be chakras, motivations, vitamins, life challenges, courses of action, books, locations or just about anything that you can dream up.

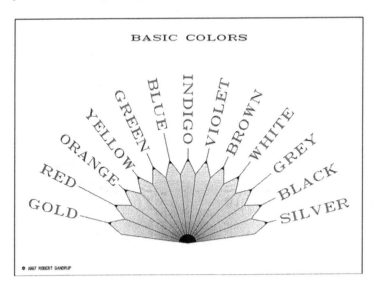

MULTIPLE FAN CHART

I made the following chart for locating usable underground water sources. I've included it here to show how these charts can be used for a specific purpose.

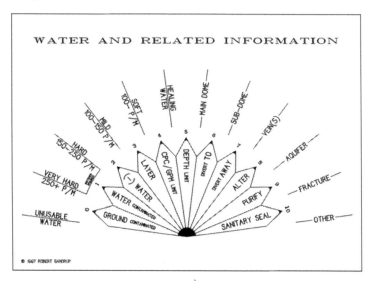

Notice that the outer portion covers the quality of the water and its possible source. The inner part is other pertinent information.

There's a lot more to water dowsing than this chart shows. Before you commit thousands of dollars to drill a well, it may be a good idea to talk to an experienced water dowser. In addition, there may local regulations or legal considerations that are specific to your area. These factors must be addressed, as well.

CIRCULAR CHART

My wife asked me to make this chart for her when she was working as a real estate broker.

Before she went to list a home, she would dowse for potential problem areas. This way she would know what questions to ask the seller and where to look. She would also have a rough idea of the potential market value. Also, there were no surprises when she saw the home/or termite inspection reports.

To use this chart, she would just turn it sideways and use either side as a fan chart. This type of chart is useful when you have too much information for one fan chart and don't want to drag around a bunch of separate ones.

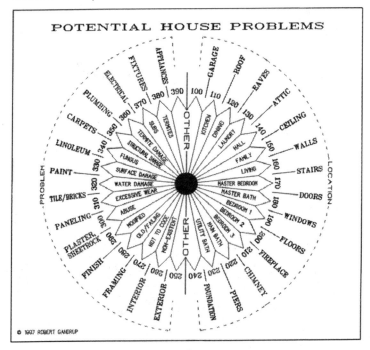

POTENTIAL HOUSE PROBLEMS

© 1997 ROBERT GANDRUP

43

The following charts are blank and can be used for just about anything. You can copy them, make your own using these as ideas or just fill them in with your own information. They're a bit small for most people but If you photocopy them, you can enlarge them at the same time. They were originally made on letter-sized paper.

BLANK 1 to 10 FAN CHART

The numbers are useful for determining percentages or any other counting you may want to do. If you need larger or smaller numbers, just mentally move the decimal place. Then 1 becomes .1, 10, 100 and so on.

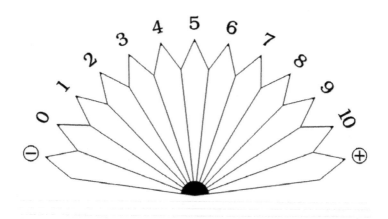

If you need more space than the petals offer, you can write out between the numbers like on the *Water and Related Information* chart. This chart has "+" and "-" signs on it. They are useful for times when you need to know whether to increase or decrease (or add / delete) something.

BLANK –5 to +5 CHART

On this chart, the numbers range from –5 to +5. This is useful for determining the overall benefit of what you are dowsing. For example, is something in your life beneficial or non-beneficial for you? When considering a change, it's good to know what kind of effect it may have.

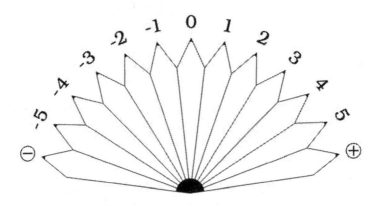

This type of dowsing can be used for in many ways. I've used it to determine how something is affecting my life, how satisfied I would be with a new purchase, the overall benefit of making any manner of changes including attitude or thought processes (yes, we all have complete control over our choices with this) or any number of other uses.

Final Tip on Charts:
You can save a lot of time by making master charts. In my stash of charts, I have one that lists my other charts on spiritual growth.

NOTES

Made in the USA
San Bernardino, CA
15 March 2020

65699045R00029